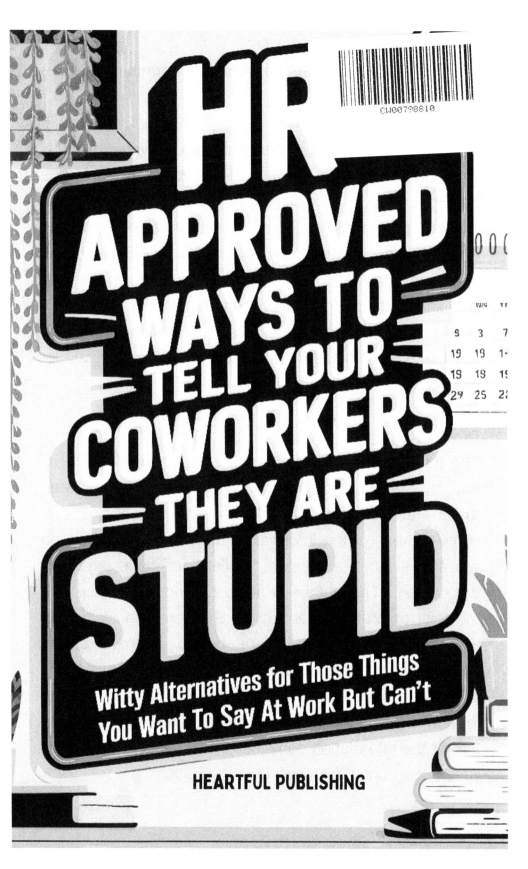

HR APPROVED WAYS TO TELL YOUR COWORKERS THEY ARE STUPID

Witty Alternatives for Those Things You Want To Say At Work But Can't

HEARTFUL PUBLISHING

HR DISCLAIMER

Welcome to HR Approved Ways to Tell Coworkers They're Stupid! Before we dive in, let's be clear: this book was crafted with humor in mind, not as an official HR handbook (our legal team insisted we say that). While our witty quips and phrases may hit close to home, we assure you they're not meant for actual workplace interactions—unless you enjoy spontaneous meetings with real HR. This book is best enjoyed as a delightful release for those thoughts you wish you could say out loud.

Read responsibly, laugh often, and remember: our "HR-approved" humor is a tool for your entertainment, not your career advancement.

Enjoy the ride!

What I Really Want To Say:

Damn it, did you seriously just screw that up again?

 HR Approved Alternative:

Let's review this task together to ensure accuracy and prevent future errors.

What I Really Want To Say:

Oh, fantastic! Another one of your brilliant blunders.

 HR Approved Alternative:

I appreciate your effort. Let's work on refining this to achieve better results.

What I Really Want To Say:

Seriously, how hard is it to follow simple fucking instructions?

 HR Approved Alternative:

Let's go over the instructions together to ensure we're on the same page.

What I Really Want To Say:

Great job—if the goal was to make things more complicated.

 HR Approved Alternative:

Thank you for your input. Let's streamline this process to enhance efficiency.

What I Really Want To Say:

You're as useful as a screen door on a submarine.

 HR Approved Alternative:

Let's coordinate our efforts to ensure we're supporting each other effectively.

What I Really Want To Say:

If ignorance is bliss, you must be the happiest person here.

 HR Approved Alternative:

There's always room for learning and growth. Let's identify areas for development.

What I Really Want To Say:

Your logic is about as clear as mud.

 HR Approved Alternative:

Can we review the reasoning behind this approach to ensure clarity?

What I Really Want To Say:

I'd explain it to you, but I left my crayons at home.

 HR Approved Alternative:

Let me provide a more detailed explanation to ensure understanding.

What I Really Want To Say:

You're the reason we have instructions.

 HR Approved Alternative:

Following guidelines closely can help us achieve better results.

What I Really Want To Say:

Are you naturally this dumb, or do you practice?

 HR Approved Alternative:

I can see there's room for improvement in this area. Let's focus on finding ways to elevate our performance.

What I Really Want To Say:

> **If I had a dollar for every time you screwed up, I'd be rich**

 HR Approved Alternative:

It seems like we've encountered some challenges recently. Let's review how we can avoid similar issues moving forward.

What I Really Want To Say:

I didn't realize we were in the business of lowering standards

 HR Approved Alternative:

It's always important to aim high. We should revisit our approach to ensure we're meeting expectations

What I Really Want To Say:

You must be the reason we have a manual for everything

 HR Approved Alternative:

Your attention to detail is valuable, but we might benefit from clarifying processes to avoid confusion

What I Really Want To Say:

Wow, you broke it again.
Impressive.

 HR Approved Alternative:

It seems we've run into another issue. Let's troubleshoot and find a way to prevent this from happening again

What I Really Want To Say:

Every time you speak, a brain cell dies.

 HR Approved Alternative:

Let's take a moment to clarify your thoughts so we can move forward with a clear understanding.

What I Really Want To Say:

Your ideas are like expired coupons—useless

 HR Approved Alternative:

There's definitely potential in your idea, but I think it could benefit from some refinement.

What I Really Want To Say:

Why use a brain when you can just wing it, right?

 HR Approved Alternative:

Planning ahead can help avoid unexpected issues. Let's discuss how we can be better prepared next time

What I Really Want To Say:

That's the dumbest thing I've heard today, and I've been on the phone with tech support.

 HR Approved Alternative:

There's some confusion here, let's regroup and make sure everyone is on the same page

What I Really Want To Say:

Is your brain a Windows 95 running in Safe Mode?

 HR Approved Alternative:

It seems we're working through some outdated methods. Let's look into more efficient approaches

What I Really Want To Say:

It's amazing you've made it this far in life without instructions

 HR Approved Alternative:

You've shown an ability to adapt, but having a clear plan could help improve consistency.

What I Really Want To Say:

Your work ethic is an inspiration... to slackers everywhere.

 HR Approved Alternative:

I think we can work on creating more structure and accountability to boost productivity.

What I Really Want To Say:

You're not stupid. You just have bad luck thinking

 HR Approved Alternative:

There's potential here, but let's take some time to refine the thought process behind this

What I Really Want To Say:

Are you an experiment in human patience?

 HR Approved Alternative:

Your unique approach certainly tests our resilience. Let's find a way to streamline the process.

What I Really Want To Say:

It's not that I don't like you. It's just that I don't like you.

 HR Approved Alternative:

We seem to have different working styles. Let's focus on finding common ground for collaboration

What I Really Want To Say:

Oh, look! The village idiot is in charge

 HR Approved Alternative:

It seems like we've encountered a leadership challenge. Let's find ways to align our goals more effectively

What I Really Want To Say:

You have the right to remain
silent, please use it.

 HR Approved Alternative:

Perhaps now would be a good time
to let others weigh in on the
discussion

What I Really Want To Say:

Your stupidity is giving me a headache

 HR Approved Alternative:

There's a lot to unpack here. Let's take a moment to regroup and re-evaluate the situation

What I Really Want To Say:

i'm not saying you're the worst, but you're definitely not the best.

 HR Approved Alternative:

There's always room for growth and improvement. Let's work on reaching the next level.

What I Really Want To Say:

You're like a cloud. When you disappear, it's a beautiful day.

 HR Approved Alternative:

I think we might work better independently on this task to maximize efficiency.

What I Really Want To Say:

You're like a speed bump—slowing everything down for no reason.

 HR Approved Alternative:

We could explore ways to streamline our process for quicker results.

What I Really Want To Say:

You're as bright as a black hole, and twice as dense

 HR Approved Alternative:

It seems we might be missing some key details. Let's review together to fill in the gaps.

What I Really Want To Say:

Your elevator doesn't reach the top floor, does it?

 HR Approved Alternative:

There may be some areas of understanding we need to improve. Let's address those.

What I Really Want To Say:

You're the human embodiment of a 404 error.

 HR Approved Alternative:

It seems like there's a disconnect here. Let's troubleshoot and realign our focus to avoid confusion.

What I Really Want To Say:

I'm impressed by your constant ability to lower the bar.

 HR Approved Alternative:

There's an opportunity here to raise our standards and improve the outcome.

What I Really Want To Say:

You have a face for radio and a brain for reality TV.

 HR Approved Alternative:

Your perspective definitely brings something unique to the table.

What I Really Want To Say:

Are you sure you're not just an NPC in real life?

 HR Approved Alternative:

Sometimes your work can fly under the radar. Let's find ways to bring it to the forefront.

What I Really Want To Say:

If common sense were a superpower, you'd be powerless.

 HR Approved Alternative:

There's always room to enhance our practical decision-making skills. Let's work on that.

What I Really Want To Say:

You're like a misfire in an engine—totally off and causing damage.

 HR Approved Alternative:

It looks like there's a misalignment we need to address to prevent future issues.

What I Really Want To Say:

The gene pool could use a lifeguard.

 HR Approved Alternative:

As a team, there are areas where we can definitely improve and evolve.

What I Really Want To Say:

You should wear a sign that says, 'I'm not good under pressure.'

 HR Approved Alternative:

Managing stress can be challenging, but we can work on developing better coping mechanisms.

What I Really Want To Say:

You're living proof that even a broken clock is right twice a day.

 HR Approved Alternative:

Even when things don't always go as planned, you still manage to find the solution eventually.

What I Really Want To Say:

You're like a tornado in a trailer park—always causing chaos.

 HR Approved Alternative:

Your energy is definitely contagious, but we may need to channel it into more focused efforts.

What I Really Want To Say:

I've met smarter sandwiches.

 HR Approved Alternative:

You're a work in progress, and we can continue to grow together toward more effective results.

What I Really Want To Say:

Your potential is like Bigfoot—rumored but never proven

 HR Approved Alternative:

You've got great potential, and we'll work together to help you unlock it.

What I Really Want To Say:

You're a great argument for natural selection.

 HR Approved Alternative:

Everyone has different strengths, and yours may still be emerging. Let's focus on finding them.

What I Really Want To Say:

If I rolled my eyes any harder, I'd see my brain.

 HR Approved Alternative:

It seems we have some differing perspectives here. Let's work on aligning them.

What I Really Want To Say:

It's like you were born on the highway, because that's where most accidents happen.

 HR Approved Alternative:

We may need to course-correct to ensure better outcomes moving forward.

What I Really Want To Say:

Wow, you're about as sharp as a marble

 HR Approved Alternative:

I think there's room for us to sharpen our approach and focus on more precise work.

What I Really Want To Say:

Do you ever stop to think, or is that asking too much?

 HR Approved Alternative:

Taking a moment to reflect before proceeding can often lead to better results.

What I Really Want To Say:

You're proof that evolution can go in reverse.

 HR Approved Alternative:

Everyone evolves at their own pace. Let's work together to make progress more consistently.

What I Really Want To Say:

You're slower than a dial-up connection in 1999.

 HR Approved Alternative:

There's definitely an opportunity to improve our speed and efficiency moving forward.

What I Really Want To Say:

You have the brainpower of a baked potato.

 HR Approved Alternative:

I think we can work on enhancing our problem-solving skills as a team.

What I Really Want To Say:

Your brain is like a web browser —too many tabs open, none of them working.

 HR Approved Alternative:

It seems like there's a lot going on. Let's focus on prioritizing the most important tasks.

What I Really Want To Say:

You bring everyone so much joy... when you leave the room.

 HR Approved Alternative:

I think we might work more productively when we divide responsibilities and work independently

What I Really Want To Say:

Are you always this stupid, or are you just making an extra effort today?

 HR Approved Alternative:

We all have off days. Let's try to refocus and get back on track

What I Really Want To Say:

I'm not sure if I should be impressed or concerned by your lack of competence.

 HR Approved Alternative:

It seems like there's some room for skill development here. Let's work on addressing that.

What I Really Want To Say:

You remind me of a software update—always interrupting and never actually fixing anything.

 HR Approved Alternative:

Sometimes it's important to ensure our contributions are adding value rather than causing disruptions.

What I Really Want To Say:

If stupidity were a currency, you'd be a billionaire.

 HR Approved Alternative:

There are definitely some opportunities for improvement that we can focus on to maximize your potential.

What I Really Want To Say:

You're a walking argument for the invention of spell check.

 HR Approved Alternative:

Attention to detail is important. Let's work on ensuring accuracy moving forward.

What I Really Want To Say:

I'd agree with you, but then we'd both be wrong.

 HR Approved Alternative:

It sounds like we may need to come to a more informed agreement. Let's review the facts.

What I Really Want To Say:

You have the organizational skills of a tornado.

 HR Approved Alternative:

It might help to implement more structured organization techniques for better results.

What I Really Want To Say:

Congratulations, you've set a new standard for mediocrity.

 HR Approved Alternative:

It's important that we continue to raise the bar and aim for higher standards.

What I Really Want To Say:

If ignorance is bliss, you must be the happiest person alive.

 HR Approved Alternative:

Gaining more knowledge and staying informed can definitely help us reach better outcomes.

What I Really Want To Say:

Are you intentionally this dumb, or is it just a talent?

 HR Approved Alternative:

Let's work on improving our problem-solving strategies to prevent these issues in the future.

What I Really Want To Say:

How do you manage to screw up so consistently? It's almost impressive.

 HR Approved Alternative:

We can learn from these mistakes to ensure more consistent performance moving forward.

What I Really Want To Say:

I'd suggest you go outside and get some fresh air, but I don't think nature can fix that.

 HR Approved Alternative:

Sometimes a break can provide a fresh perspective, but we also need to focus on the root cause of the issue.

What I Really Want To Say:

If you were any slower, you'd be in reverse.

 HR Approved Alternative:

We may need to focus on increasing our speed and efficiency to meet deadlines more effectively.

What I Really Want To Say:

You're like a participation trophy —completely unnecessary but here anyway.

 HR Approved Alternative:

Everyone brings value to the team, but we can always find ways to contribute more meaningfully.

What I Really Want To Say:

I didn't know we were aiming for the lowest common denominator today

 HR Approved Alternative:

It's important to aim higher and strive for better outcomes in everything we do.

What I Really Want To Say:

Your ideas are like socks with sandals—completely wrong.

 HR Approved Alternative:

It's always great to see creative thinking, but let's refine this idea for better alignment with our goals.

73

What I Really Want To Say:

You have the emotional intelligence of a rock.

 HR Approved Alternative:

Emotional intelligence is key in the workplace. Let's focus on improving communication and empathy.

What I Really Want To Say:

You're like a Wi-Fi signal in a storm—completely unreliable

 HR Approved Alternative:

Consistency is important. Let's find ways to ensure more dependable contributions in the future.

What I Really Want To Say:

You're proof that the lights are on, but nobody's home.

 HR Approved Alternative:

There are times when clarity of focus is needed. Let's work on improving that together.

What I Really Want To Say:

You have the problem-solving ability of a toddler.

 HR Approved Alternative:

Problem-solving is a skill that can always be improved. Let's focus on developing that further.

What I Really Want To Say:

You're a few fries short of a Happy Meal.

 HR Approved Alternative:

There are some areas where we can improve to ensure a more complete understanding of the tasks at hand.

What I Really Want To Say:

You're like a software bug— annoying and hard to get rid of.

 HR Approved Alternative:

Sometimes our contributions can cause friction. Let's work on making our impact more positive.

What I Really Want To Say:

I'm surprised you manage to dress yourself in the morning.

 HR Approved Alternative:

Independence is important, but we can all benefit from asking for help when necessary to achieve the best results.

What I Really Want To Say:

You're more confused than a chameleon in a bag of Skittles.

 HR Approved Alternative:

It seems like there's some confusion here. Let's clarify and realign our understanding.

What I Really Want To Say:

You're the human equivalent of a participation award.

 HR Approved Alternative:

Everyone contributes in their own way, but we can work on finding ways to add more meaningful value.

What I Really Want To Say:

You're about as useful as a chocolate teapot.

 HR Approved Alternative:

Let's find a role where your skills can be better utilized for more effective results.

What I Really Want To Say:

I'd tell you to think before you speak, but I doubt it would help.

 HR Approved Alternative:

Thoughtful communication can often prevent misunderstandings. Let's work on that together.

What I Really Want To Say:

You're like a broken pencil— completely pointless.

 HR Approved Alternative:

There's value in everything we do, but let's focus on how we can make our work more impactful.

What I Really Want To Say:

If brains were dynamite, you wouldn't have enough to blow your nose.

 ## HR Approved Alternative:

Intellectual growth is always possible. Let's focus on expanding our knowledge base moving forward.

What I Really Want To Say:

You couldn't pour water out of a boot if the instructions were on the heel.

 HR Approved Alternative:

Attention to detail is key in completing tasks accurately. Let's work on improving that.

What I Really Want To Say:

I'd call you a tool, but that would imply you're useful.

 HR Approved Alternative:

Everyone has value, but we can work on finding where you can be most effective.

What I Really Want To Say:

**You're slower than a turtle
running through peanut butter.**

 HR Approved Alternative:

We may need to focus on increasing
our efficiency to meet deadlines
more effectively.

What I Really Want To Say:

:If your brain was any smaller, it would be a marble.

 HR Approved Alternative:

Intellectual growth is a continuous process. Let's focus on further development.

What I Really Want To Say:

You're more lost than a tourist in Times Square.

 HR Approved Alternative:

There's definitely some confusion here. Let's take time to clarify and ensure we're all on the same page.

What I Really Want To Say:

You're as reliable as a flip phone in 2024.

 HR Approved Alternative:

Consistency and reliability are key. Let's work on improving those aspects moving forward.

What I Really Want To Say:

You're like a fire drill— chaos without any real danger.

 HR Approved Alternative:

Your energy is valuable, but we might need to channel it more productively.

What I Really Want To Say:

You're like a seatbelt on a motorcycle–completely unnecessary.

 HR Approved Alternative:

Sometimes our contributions may not be immediately needed, but we can always find a way to add value.

What I Really Want To Say:

You're like a reverse lottery—you never win.

 HR Approved Alternative:

Sometimes things don't go as planned, but there's always room for improvement moving forward.

What I Really Want To Say:

You're slower than dial-up internet.

 HR Approved Alternative:

Efficiency is key. Let's work on increasing our speed to meet the demands of the project.

What I Really Want To Say:

You're as confusing as IKEA instructions without the pictures.

 HR Approved Alternative:

It seems there's some miscommunication here. Let's clarify and ensure everyone's on the same page.

What I Really Want To Say:

If brains were taxed, you'd get a refund.

 ## HR Approved Alternative:

There's always room to expand our knowledge base. Let's focus on continuous learning.

What I Really Want To Say:

You're like an appendix—no one knows what you're here for.

 HR Approved Alternative:

Let's reassess your role to ensure it's aligned with the team's goals and objectives.

What I Really Want To Say:

You're slower than paint drying in winter.

 HR Approved Alternative:

Increasing efficiency is key to meeting our deadlines. Let's focus on improving that.

What I Really Want To Say:

If brains were sold by weight, you'd be the discount bin.

 HR Approved Alternative:

We can always focus on expanding our knowledge base and improving our problem-solving skills.

What I Really Want To Say:

You're like a square wheel—completely useless but oddly fascinating.

 HR Approved Alternative:

Sometimes we need to reassess our approach to ensure it aligns with the goals of the team.

What I Really Want To Say:

You're like an out-of-tune piano—completely off-key.

 HR Approved Alternative:

It seems like there's some misalignment here. Let's work together to ensure we're all in sync.

www.ingramcontent.com/pod-product-compliance
Lightning Source LLC
LaVergne TN
LVHW021739151224
799183LV00038B/562

9 7 9 8 3 4 5 0 3 7 9 5 9